Contents

Introduction 2
Essential Maya Angelou Quotes 9
Short and Pithy Quotes 12
Inspirational and Uplifting Quotes .... .14
Wise and Enlightening Quotes 17
Deep and Profound Quotes 19
Quotes about Love, Self-Love, and Relationships 21
Quotes about Life 24
Funny Maya Quotes 26
Quotes about Gratitude and Happiness 28
Quotes about Courage and Success 30
Quotes about Family 33
Quotes about Friendship 35
Quotes about Feminism and Womanhood 37
Quotes about God and Religion 41
Quotes about History and Racism 42
Quotes about Justice and 'Doing the Right Thing' 45
Selected Lines from Poems 48
Selected Quotes from Books and Literature 50

INTRODUCTION

Maya Angelou was a poet and award-winning author known for her acclaimed memoir I Know Why the Caged Bird Sings and her numerous poetry and essay collections.

Who Was Maya Angelou?

Marguerite Annie Johnson Angelou (April 4, 1928 to May 28, 2014), known as Maya Angelou, was an American author, actress, screenwriter, dancer, poet and civil rights activist best known for her 1969 memoir, I Know Why the Caged Bird Sings, which made literary history as the first nonfiction best-seller by an African-American woman. Angelou received several honors throughout her career, including two NAACP Image Awards in the outstanding literary work (nonfiction) category, in 2005 and 2009.

Maya Angelou's Poetry

'Just Give Me a Cool Drink of Water 'Fore I Die' (1971)

- Angelou published several collections of poetry, but her most famous was 1971's collection Just Give Me a Cool Drink of Water 'Fore I Die, which was nominated for the Pulitzer Prize.

'On the Pulse of Morning'

- One of her most famous works, Angelou wrote this poem especially for and recited at President Bill Clinton's inaugural ceremony in January 1993. The occasion marked the first inaugural recitation since 1961, when Robert Frost delivered his poem "The Gift Outright" at President John F. Kennedy's inauguration. Angelou went on to win a Grammy Award (best spoken word album) for the audio version of the poem.

Maya Angelou's Books

'I Know Why the Caged Bird Sings' (1969)

- Friend and fellow writer James Baldwin urged Angelou to write about her life experiences, resulting in the enormously successful 1969 memoir about her childhood and young adult years, I Know Why the Caged Bird Sings. The poignant story made literary history as the first nonfiction best-seller by an African-American woman. The book, which made Angelou an international star, continues to be regarded as her most popular autobiographical work. In 1995, Angelou was lauded for remaining on The New York Times' paperback nonfiction best-seller list for two years—the longest-running record in the chart's history.

'All God's Children Need Traveling Shoes' (1986)

- A lyrical exploration about of what it means to be an African American in Africa, this autobiographical book covers the years Angelou spent living in Ghana.

'Wouldn't Take Nothing for My Journey Now' (1994)

- This inspirational essay collection features Angelou's insights about spirituality and living well.

'A Song Flung Up to Heaven' (2002)

- Another autobiographical work, A Song Flung Up to Heaven explores Angelou's return from Africa to the U.S. and her ensuing struggle to cope with the devastating assassinations of two human rights leaders with whom she worked,

Malcolm X and Martin Luther King Jr. The book ends when, at the encouragement of her friend James Baldwin, Angelou began work on I Know Why the Caged Bird Sings.

'Letter to My Daughter' (2008)

- Dedicated to the daughter Angelou never had, this book of essays features Angelou's advice for young women about living a life of meaning.

Cookbooks

- Interested in health, Angelou's published cookbooks include Hallelujah! The Welcome Table: A Lifetime of Memories With Recipes (2005) and Great Food, All Day Long (2010).

Death

After experiencing health issues for a number of years, Maya Angelou died on May 28, 2014, at her home in Winston-Salem, North Carolina. The news of her passing spread quickly with many people taking to social media to mourn and remember Angelou. Singer Mary J. Blige and politician Cory Booker were among those who tweeted their favorite quotes by her in tribute. President Barack Obama also issued a statement about Angelou, calling her "a brilliant writer, a fierce friend, and a truly phenomenal woman." Angelou "had the ability to remind us that we are all God's children; that we all have something to offer," he wrote.

Angelou's Son and Husbands

In 1944, a 16-year-old Angelou gave birth to a son, Guy (a short-lived high school relationship led to the pregnancy). A poet himself, Angelou's son now goes by the name Guy Johnson.

In 1952, the future literary icon wed Anastasios Angelopulos, a Greek sailor from whom she took her professional name — a blend of her childhood nickname, "Maya," and a shortened version of his surname. The couple later divorced. Notoriously secretive about her marriages, Angelou was likely married at least three times, including in 1973 to a carpenter, Paul du Feu.

When and Where Was Maya Angelou Born?

Maya Angelou was born on April 4, 1928, in St. Louis, Missouri.

Family, Early Life and Education

Angelou had a difficult childhood. Her parents split up when she was very young, and she and her older brother, Bailey, were sent to live with their father's mother, Anne Henderson, in Stamps, Arkansas.

As an African American, Angelou experienced firsthand racial prejudices and discrimination in Arkansas. She also suffered at the hands of a family associate around the age of seven: During a visit with her mother, Angelou was raped by her mother's boyfriend. Then, as vengeance for the sexual assault, Angelou's uncles killed the boyfriend. So traumatized by the experience, Angelou stopped talking. She returned to Arkansas and spent years as a virtual mute.

During World War II, Angelou moved to San Francisco, California, where she won a scholarship to study dance and acting at the California Labor School. Also during this time, Angelou became the first black female cable car conductor — a job she held only briefly

— in San Francisco. After giving birth to her son, she worked a number of jobs to support herself and her child.

Acting and Singing Career

In the mid-1950s, Angelou's career as a performer began to take off. She landed a role in a touring production of Porgy and Bess, later appearing in the off-Broadway production Calypso Heat Wave (1957) and releasing her first album, Miss Calypso (1957). A member of the Harlem Writers Guild and a civil rights activist, Angelou organized and starred in the musical revue Cabaret for Freedom as a benefit for the Southern Christian Leadership Conference, also serving as the SCLC's northern coordinator.

In 1961, Angelou appeared in an off-Broadway production of Jean Genet's The Blacks with James Earl Jones, Lou Gossett Jr. and Cicely Tyson.

Angelou went on to earn a Tony Award nomination for her role in the play Look Away (1973) and an Emmy Award nomination for her work on the television miniseries Roots (1977), among other honors.

Time in Africa

Angelou spent much of the 1960s abroad, living first in Egypt and then in Ghana, working as an editor and a freelance writer. Angelou also held a position at the University of Ghana for a time. In Ghana she also joined a community of "Revolutionist Returnees" exploring pan-Africanism and became close with human rights activist and black nationalist leader Malcolm X. In 1964, on returning to the U.S., she helped him set up the Organization of Afro-American Unity, which disbanded after Malcolm X's assassination the following year.

Screenplay Author and Director

After publishing Caged Bird, Angelou broke new ground artistically, educationally and socially with her drama Georgia, Georgia in 1972, which made her the first African-American woman to have her screenplay produced.

In 1998, seeking new creative challenges, Angelou made her directorial debut with Down in the Delta, starring Alfre Woodard.

Other Awards

Angelou's career has seen numerous accolades, including the Chicago International Film Festival's 1998 Audience Choice Award and a nod from the Acapulco Black Film Festival in 1999 for Down in the Delta. She also won two NAACP Image Awards in the outstanding literary work (nonfiction) category, for her 2005 cookbook and 2008's Letter to My Daughter.

Personal Life

Martin Luther King Jr., a close friend of Angelou's, was assassinated on her birthday (April 4) in 1968. Angelou stopped celebrating her birthday for years afterward, and sent flowers to King's widow, Coretta Scott King, for more than 30 years, until Coretta's death in 2006.

Angelou was also good friends with TV personality Oprah Winfrey, who organized several birthday celebrations for the award-winning author, including a week-long cruise for her 70th birthday in 1998.

*

Essential Maya Angelou Quotes

Ask for what you want and be prepared to get it!

Do the best you can until you know better. Then when you know better, do better.

Hate, it has caused a lot of problems in the world, but has not solved one yet. (This is one of my favorite Maya Angelou quote. Leave a reply here and let me know what's yours!)

I love to see a young girl go out and grab the world by the lapels. Life's a bitch. You've got to go out and kick ass.

I not only have the right to stand up for myself, but I have the responsibility. I can't ask somebody else to stand up for me if I won't stand up for myself. And once you stand up for yourself, you'd be surprised that people say, "Can I be of help?".

I was told many years ago by my grandmother who raised me: If somebody puts you on a road and you don't feel comfortable on it and you look ahead and you don't like the destination and you look behind and you don't want to return to that place, step off the road.

I've learned that people will forget what you said, people will forget what you did, but people will never forget how you made them feel.

If you don't like something, change it. If you can't change it, change your attitude.

Life is not measured by the number of breaths we take, but by the moments that take our breath away.

My great blessing is my son, but I have daughters. I have white ones and Black ones and fat ones and thin ones and pretty ones and plain. I have gay ones and straight. I have daughters. I have Asian ones, I have Jewish ones, I have Muslim ones.

My work is to be honest. My work is to try to think clearly, then have the courage to make sure that what I say is the truth.

Success is liking yourself, liking what you do, and liking how you do it.

The children to whom we read simple stories may or may not show gratitude, but each boon we give strengthens the pillars of the world.

We may encounter many defeats but we must not be defeated.

When you know you are of worth, you don't have to raise your voice, you don't have to become rude, you don't have to become vulgar; you just are. And you are like the sky is, as the air is, the same way water is wet. It doesn't have to protest.

You alone are enough. You have nothing to prove to anybody.

You can only become truly accomplished at something you love. Don't make money your goal. Instead, pursue the things you love doing, and then do them so well that people can't take their eyes off you.

You can't really know where you are going until you know where you have been.

You can't use up creativity. The more you use, the more you have.

Short and Pithy Quotes

Achievement brings its own anticlimax.

All great achievements require time.

Be a rainbow in someone else's cloud.

Determine to live life with flair and laughter.

Effective action is always unjust.

Everybody is worth everything.

I believe that every person is born with talent.

I know why the caged bird sings.

If someone shows you who they really are, believe them.

Life loves the liver of it.

Nothing will work unless you do.

Surviving is important. Thriving is elegant.

The honorary duty of a human being is to love.

The need for change bulldozed a road down the center of my mind.

The needs of society determine its ethics.

We need much less than we think we need.

When you learn, teach, when you get, give.

Whining is just unbecoming.

Your belief and your work will speak for you.

Inspirational and Uplifting Quotes

All men are prepared to accomplish the incredible if their ideals are threatened.

How important it is for us to recognize and celebrate our heroes and she-roes!

I long, as does every human being, to be at home wherever I find myself.

I want all my senses engaged. Let me absorb the world's variety and uniqueness.

I'm really saddened by the attempts to separate and polarize. This is a time when we have hungry people, people out of work, and people out of spirit. This is a time where we need to uplift, not to separate.

I've learned that no matter what happens, or how bad it seems today, life does go on, and it will be better tomorrow.

If a human being dreams a great dream, dares to love somebody; if a human being dares to be Martin King, or Mahatma Gandhi, or Mother Theresa, or Malcolm X; if a human being dares to be bigger than the condition into which she or he was born – it means so can you. And so you can try to stretch, stretch, stretch yourself so you can internalize, 'Homo sum, humani nil a me alienum puto. I am a human being, nothing human can be alien to me.' That's one thing I'm learning.

If one is lucky, a solitary fantasy can totally transform one million realities.

It's very important to know the neighbor next door and the people down the street and the people in another race.

Look what you've already come through! Don't deny it. You've already come through some things, which are very painful. If you've been alive until you're 35, you have gone through some pain. It cost you something. And you've come through it. So at least look at that. And have a sense to look at yourself and say, "Well, wait a minute. I'm stronger than I thought I was.

My great hope is to laugh as much as I cry; to get my work done and try to love somebody and have the courage to accept the love in return.

My wish for you is that you continue. Continue to be who and how you are, to astonish a mean world with your acts of kindness.

On what she feels about the world today: I feel very hopeful, very expectant. I'm looking forward to it.

One isn't necessarily born with courage, but one is born with potential. Without courage, we cannot practice any other virtue with consistency. We can't be kind, true, merciful, generous, or honest.

Someone was hurt before you, wronged before you, hungry before you, frightened before you, beaten before you, humiliated before you, raped before you... yet, someone survived... You can do anything you choose to do.

The idea is to write it so that people hear it and it slides through the brain and goes straight to the heart.

There is no greater agony than bearing an untold story inside you.

We need to not be in denial about what we've done, what we've come through. It will help us if we all do that.

When I forgive other people, I let them go, I free them from my ignorance. And as soon as I do, I feel lighter, brighter and better.

You should be angry. You must not be bitter. Bitterness is like cancer. It eats upon the host. It doesn't do anything to the object of its displeasure. So use that anger. You write it. You paint it. You dance it. You march it. You vote it. You do everything about it. You talk it. Never stop talking it.

Wise and Enlightening Quotes

A leader sees greatness in other people. He nor she can be much of a leader if all she sees is herself.

Bitterness is like cancer. It eats upon the host. But anger is like fire. It burns it all clean.

I do my best because I'm counting on you counting on me.

I like to go back and read poems that I wrote fifty years ago, twenty years ago, and sometimes they surprise me – I didn't know I knew that then. Or maybe I didn't know it then, and I know more now.

I've learned that forgiving is one of the greatest gifts that I can give myself.

I've learned that making a "living" is not the same thing as making a "life."

I've learned that you shouldn't go through life with a catcher's mitt on both hands; you need to be able to throw something back.

I've learned that even when I have pains, I don't have to be one.

If you are always trying to be normal you will never know how amazing you can be.

My mother said I must always be intolerant of ignorance but

understanding of illiteracy.

Never make someone a priority when all you are to them is an option.

Seek patience and passion in equal amounts. Patience alone will not build the temple. Passion alone will destroy its walls.

We delight in the beauty of the butterfly, but rarely admit the changes it has gone through to achieve that beauty.

Deep and Profound Quotes

A woman's heart should be so hidden in God that a man has to seek Him just to find her.

Everything in the universe has a rhythm, everything dances.

Grace is like a lake of drinkable water right outside your door. But you stay inside and die of thirst.

If you want what you're saying heard, then take your time and say it so that the listener will actually hear it. You might save somebody's life. Your own, first.

Listen to yourself and in that quietude you might hear the voice of God.

Nobody can enjoy unless we all enjoy, truly enjoy.

Since time is the one immaterial object which we cannot influence, neither speed up nor slow down, add to nor diminish, it is an imponderably valuable gift.

We are not just flesh and blood. And our hungers are not going to be set aside as just flesh and blood.

We are only as blind as we want to be.

You can ask forgiveness of others, but in the end the real forgiveness is in one's own self.

Quotes about Love, Self-Love, and Relationships

By love I don't mean indulgence. I do not mean sentimentality. And in this instance, I don't even mean romance. I mean that condition that allowed humans to dream of God. That condition that allowed the "dumb" to write spirituals and Russian songs and Irish lilts. That is love, and it's so much larger than anything I can conceive.

First best is falling in love. Second best is being in love. Least best is falling out of love. But any of it is better than never having been in love.

Forgiveness is a gift you give yourself.

Forgiveness. It's one of the greatest gifts you can give yourself, to forgive. Forgive everybody. You are relieved of carrying that burden of resentment. You really are lighter. You feel lighter. You just drop that.

Have enough courage to trust love one more time and always one more time.

I believe that people want the scent of love, more than anything else. And I don't mean sentimentality, I don't mean mush. I mean that idea, that human beings are more alike than we are different.

I have found that among its other benefits, giving liberates the soul of the giver.

I'm convinced that the negative has power. It lives. And if you allow it to perch in your house, in your mind, in your life, it can take you over. So when the rude or cruel thing is said – the lambasting, the gay bashing, the hate – I say, "Take it all out of my house!" Those negative words climb into the woodwork and into the furniture, and the next thing you know they'll be on my skin.

If I am not good to myself, how can I expect anyone else to be good to me?

If we lose love and self-respect for each other, this is how we finally die.

If you find it in your heart to care for somebody else, you will have succeeded.

If you happen to fall in love with someone in another race, it's more difficult, because you have to translate yourself.

If you want to liberate someone, love them. Not be in love with them – that's dangerous.

It's hard because people think they have something to lose and the truth is they have everything to gain in trying to love somebody.

It's very hard for adults to maintain respect and romance so that a love affair can be sustained over years.

Love is like a virus. It can happen to anybody at any time.

Love recognizes no barriers. It jumps hurdles, leaps fences, penetrates walls to arrive at its destination full of hope.

Self-pity in its early stages is as snug as a feather mattress. Only when it hardens does it become uncomfortable.

Whatever you want to do, if you want to be great at it, you have to love it and be able to make sacrifices for it.

When people see the laughing face, even if they're jealous of it, their burden is lightened. But do it first for yourself. Laugh and dare to try to love somebody, starting with yourself.

When we find someone who is brave, fun, intelligent, and loving, we have to thank the universe.

You can never be great at anything unless you love it. Not be in love with it, but love the thing, admire the thing. And it seems that if you love the thing, and you don't just want to possess it, it will find you. But if you're in love with the thing, it may run like hell away from you.

Quotes about Life

Human beings are more alike than unalike. Whether in Paris, Texas, or Paris, France, we all want to have good jobs where we are needed and respected and paid just a little more than we deserve. We want healthy children, safe streets, to be loved and have the unmitigated gall to accept love.

I believe in living a poetic life, an art full life. Everything we do from the way we raise our children to the way we welcome our friends is part of a large canvas we are creating.

I encourage courtesy. To accept nothing less than courtesy, and to give nothing less than courtesy.

I think a hero is any person really intent on making this a better place for all people.

I've learned that life sometimes gives you a second chance.

If we live long enough, we may even get over war. I imagine a time when somebody will mention the word war and everyone in the room will start to laugh. And what do you mean war?

Life is pure adventure, and the sooner we realize that, the quicker we will be able to treat life as art.

Life loves to be taken by the lapel and told, 'I'm with you kid. Let's go'.

Most people don't grow up. Most people age. They find parking spaces, honor their credit cards, get married, have children, and call that maturity. What that is, is aging.

Music was my refuge. I could crawl into the space between the notes and curl my back to loneliness.

Open your eyes to the beauty around you, open your mind to the wonders of life, open your heart to those who love you, and always be true to yourself.

There are those who say that poets should use her and his art to change the world. I'd agree with that, but I think everybody should do that. I think the chef and the baker and the candlestick maker – I think everybody should be hoping to make it a better world.

There is a very fine line between loving life and being greedy for it.

To those who have given up on love: I say, "Trust life a little bit".

We can be better, we can be wiser, we can be more kind. Yes we have to change. We have to grow up and stop acting like 10 years old. Yes there is much to do, much to see, much to go into.

We spend precious hours fearing the inevitable. It would be wise to use that time adoring our families, cherishing our friends and living our lives.

Funny Maya Quotes

I do not trust people who don't love themselves and yet tell me, 'I love you.' There is an African saying which is: Be careful when a naked person offers you a shirt.

I don't trust anyone who doesn't laugh.

I never have written every day. When I'm writing a book, I write Monday through Friday. I always try to take Saturday and pretend to have some sanity.

I've learned that you can tell a lot about a person by the way (s)he handles these three things: a rainy day, lost luggage, and tangled Christmas tree lights.

If you have only one smile in you, give it to the people you love. Don't be surly at home, then go out in the street and start grinning 'Good morning' at total strangers.

My life has been one great big joke, a dance that's walked a song that's spoke, I laugh so hard I almost choke when I think about myself.

My mission in life is not merely to survive, but to thrive; and to do so with some passion, some compassion, some humor, and some style.

Nature has no mercy at all. Nature says, 'I'm going to snow. If you have on a bikini and no snowshoes, that's tough. I am going to snow anyway.'

The best candy shop a child can be left alone in, is the library.

This is a wonderful day, I have never seen this one before.

Quotes about Gratitude and Happiness

Be present in all things and thankful for all things.

Every day I awaken I am grateful. My intent is to be totally present in that day. And laugh as much as possible.

Happiness is a chance to talk to a friend, to hear good music, to have a good glass of wine. Happiness is a chance to be myself and to find people with whom I agree or who I don't agree but I can learn something.

I have respect for the past, but I'm a person of the moment.

I try to see every day as a celebration.

I'm here, and I do my best to be completely centered at the place I'm at, then I go forward to the next place.

If you must look back, do so forgivingly. If you will look forward, do so prayerfully. But the wisest course would be to be present in the present gratefully.

It's the fire in my eyes, and the flash of my teeth, the swing in my waist, and the joy in my feet.

Joy is a freedom. It helps a person to find his or her own liberation. The person who is joyous takes responsibility for the time he/she takes up and the space that he/she occupies. You share it! Some of you have it ... you share it! That is what joy is! When you continue to give it away you will still have so much more of it.

Let gratitude be the pillow upon which you kneel to say your nightly prayer. And let faith be the bridge you build to overcome evil and welcome good.

She comprehended the perversity of life, that in the struggle lies the joy.

Stormy or sunny days, glorious or lonely nights, I maintain an attitude of gratitude.

The ache for home lives in all of us, the safe place where we can go as we are and not be questioned.

The ship of my life may or may not be sailing on calm and amiable seas. The challenging days of my existence may or may not be bright and promising. Stormy or sunny days, glorious or lonely nights, I maintain an attitude of gratitude. If I insist on being pessimistic, there is always tomorrow. Today I am blessed.

When we give cheerfully and accept gratefully, everyone is blessed.

When you wish someone joy, you wish them peace, love, prosperity, happiness... all the good things.

Quotes about Courage and Success

At fifteen life had taught me undeniably that surrender, in its place, was as honorable as resistance, especially if one had no choice.

Courage is the most important of all the virtues, because without courage you can't practice any other virtue consistently. You can practice any virtue erratically, but nothing consistently without courage.

Courage, I don't think anybody is born with courage. I think you may be born with a flair to braggadocio, you know. That's not courage.

I am not competing with anyone other than myself. I want to be excellent at whatever I do.

I believe that the most important single thing, beyond discipline and creativity is daring to dare.

I did get knocked down flat in front of the whole world, and I rose. I didn't run away – I rose right where I'd been knocked down. And then that's how you get to know yourself.

I have enough of life in me to make somebody jealous enough to want to knock me down. I have so much courage in me that I have the effrontery, the incredible gall to stand up. That's it. That's how you get to know who you are.

I think that each of us is so much alike, and yet at the same time we are so different, and I have a feeling that if you encountered difficulty, and I with my age encountered the same difficulty, I would respond one way, and you would respond another. Neither would be right or wrong. It's just that each of us is courageous, and that's what I encourage, courage, and the courage to see, and the courage to say to oneself what one has seen. Don't be in denial.

I've learned that whenever I decide something with an open heart, I usually make the right decision.

If I am going to do the most difficult and frightening thing – dying – is it possible that I could do some difficult and impossible things that are good?

If I'm here, I'll be trying to be a better human being, a better writer, a better friend and a better beloved.

If somebody is really trying to take your head off with a baseball bat – I don't know how long you're supposed to stand there and turn the other cheek, so he or she can get a better angle at taking your head off.

In order to win, we pay with energy and effort and discipline. If we lose, we pay in disappointment, discontent, and lack of fulfillment.

It is always about the work. In the latter years of your life, your happiness and your self-esteem will be determined by the mountains you surmounted, the valleys you climbed out of, and the life and/or career that you forged for yourself.

The only way you can be a mark is if you want something for nothing. If you're greedy, you're set up.

The quality of strength lined with tenderness is an unbeatable combination, as are intelligence and necessity when unblunted by formal education.

Those who have something to say accept the fact that that's lonely. One already knows that there will be adversaries.

We may encounter many defeats, but we must not be defeated. It may even be necessary to encounter the defeat, so that we can know who we are.

Whining lets the brute know there's a victim for him in the neighborhood.

You have to deal with what you encounter. But you must not be reduced. And so a way not to be reduced is don't whine! Don't let the incidents which take place in life bring you low.

You may not control all the events that happen to you, but you can decide not to be reduced by them.

You only are free when you realize you belong no place – you belong every place – no place at all. The price is high. The reward is great.

Quotes about Family

A mother's love liberates.

Home is a refuge not only from the world, but a refuge from my worries, my troubles, my concerns.

I do not believe that the accident of birth makes people sisters and brothers. It makes them siblings. Gives them mutuality of parentage. Sisterhood and brotherhood are conditions people have to work at. It's a serious matter. You compromise, you give, you take, you stand firm, and you're relentless...And it is an investment. Sisterhood means if you happen to be in Burma and I happen to be in San Diego and I'm married to someone who is very jealous and you're married to somebody who is very possessive, if you call me in the middle of the night, I have to come.

I sustain myself with the love of family.

I've learned that regardless of your relationship with your parents, you'll miss them when they're gone from your life.

If I have a monument in this world, it is my son.

My pride had been starched by a family who assumed unlimited authority in its own affairs.

The love of the family, the love of one person can heal. It heals the scars left by a larger society. A massive, powerful society.

The sisters and brothers that you meet give you the materials which your character uses to build itself. It is said that some people are born great, others achieve it, some have it thrust upon them. In truth, the ways in which your character is built have to do with all three of those. Those around you, those you choose, and those who choose you.

Quotes about Friendship

A friend may be waiting behind a stranger's face.

A man or woman who sees other people as whole and prepared and accords them respect and the same rights has arranged his or her own allies.

Each one of us has lived through some devastation, some loneliness, some weather superstorm or spiritual superstorm, when we look at each other we must say, I understand. I understand how you feel because I have been there myself. We must support each other and empathize with each other because each of us is more alike than we are unalike.

I think the more we know the better we are. I mean not just facts. The more we know about each other, the closer we are to learn something about our selves.

I think we ought to give ourselves more time. We should be more patient with ourselves and with each other.

I've learned that every day you should reach out and touch someone. People love a warm hug, or just a friendly pat on the back.

Perhaps travel cannot prevent bigotry, but by demonstrating that all peoples cry, laugh, eat, worry, and die, it can introduce the idea that if we try and understand each other, we may even become friends.

The most called-upon prerequisite of a friend is an accessible ear.

When someone shows you who they are, believe them the first time. People know themselves much better than you do. That's why it's important to stop expecting them to be something other than who they are.

Quotes about Feminism and Womanhood

A wise woman wishes to be no one's enemy; a wise woman refuses to be anyone's victim.

A woman in harmony with her spirit is like a river flowing. She goes where she will without pretense and arrives at her destination prepared to be herself and only herself.

Any book that helps a child to form a habit of reading, to make reading one of his deep and continuing needs, is good for him.

Children's talent to endure stems from their ignorance of alternatives.

Courage allows the successful woman to fail – and to learn powerful lessons from the failure – so that in the end, she didn't fail at all.

Each child belongs to all of us and they will bring us a tomorrow in direct relation to the responsibility we have shown to them.

I am a woman phenomenally, phenomenal woman that is your grandmother, that is your mother, that is your sister, that is you and that is me.

I became the kind of parent my mother was to me.

I do hope that young men and women will start to think for themselves and start to take responsibility for their own thoughts.

I have a feeling that I make a very good friend, and I'm a good mother, and a good sister, and a good citizen. I am involved in life itself – all of it. And I have a lot of energy and a lot of nerve.

I think we have systematically and critically harmed ourselves and many young people by advising them not to try things.

I've learned that I still have a lot to learn.

If a person – any human being – is told often enough, "You are nothing. You are nothing. You account for nothing. You count for nothing. You are less than a human being. I have no visibility of you", the person finally begins to believe it.

If I'm going to a new country, I try to learn something about the language and the culture, so I don't just go bumbling over things.

If the door has been opened and I've been invited, or if I'm not invited and I somehow know I'm supposed to go in there, I put myself together and go in, praying all the while. I try to learn something before I go in. I try to show some respect of the place I'm going into.

If you're in love with your children, you're in their lives all the time. Leave them alone. Let them grow and make some mistakes.

Most plain girls are virtuous because of the scarcity of opportunity to be otherwise.

My mother had said me, "All right, you've been raised, so don't let anybody else raise you. You know the difference between right and wrong. Do right. And remember – you can always come home." And she continued to liberate me until she died.

My mother is so full of joy and life. I am her child. And that is better than being the child of anyone else in the world.

My mother raised me, and then freed me.

My mother said I must always be intolerant of ignorance but understanding of illiteracy. That some people, unable to go to school, were more educated and more intelligent than college professors.

On her mother: On the night she died, I went to the hospital. I told my mom, "Let me tell you about yourself. You deserved a great daughter, and you got one. And you liberated me to be one. So if it's time for you to go, you may have done everything God brought you here to do.

On her mother: She'd talk to me as if I had some sense.

People feel guilty. And guilt is stymieing. Guilt immobilizes. Guilt closes the air ducts and the veins, and makes people ignorant.

Stepping onto a brand-new path is difficult, but not more difficult than remaining in a situation, which is not nurturing to the whole woman.

The real difficulty is to overcome how you think about yourself. If we don't have that we never grow, we never learn, and sure as hell we should never teach.

The sadness of the women's movement is that they don't allow the necessity of love. See, I don't personally trust any revolution where love is not allowed.

There is nothing so pitiful as a young cynic because he has gone from knowing nothing to believing nothing.

We need to remember to teach our children that solitude can be a much-to-be-desired condition. Not only is it acceptable to be alone; at times it is positively to be wished for.....In the silence we listen to ourselves. Then we ask questions of ourselves. We describe ourselves to ourselves, and in the quietude we may even hear the voice of God.

When teachers or people in authority put me down or in one way or another tried to make me feel less than equal to what they thought I should be – my mother was on my side. It was amazing.

Quotes about God and Religion

God puts rainbows in the clouds so that each of us – in the dreariest and most dreaded moments – can see a possibility of hope.

I believe that each of us comes from the Creator trailing wisps of glory. So at this wonderful, young age of 65, I don't know yet what the Lord has for me to do. I try to live up to the energy and to the calling, but I wouldn't dare say I have even scratched the surface yet.

I'm working at trying to be a Christian, and that's serious business. It's like trying to be a good Jew, a good Muslim, a good Buddhist, a good Shintoist, a good Zoroastrian, a good friend, a good lover, a good mother, a good buddy – it's serious business.

Stand up straight and realize who you are, that you tower over your circumstances. You are a child of God. Stand up straight.

The most difficult thing in the world, it seems to me, is to realize that I am a child of God; to keep that in my mind all the time.

While I know myself as a creation of God, I am also obligated to realize and remember that everyone else and everything else are also God's creation.

Quotes about History and Racism

All of my history as an African-American woman, as a Jewish woman, as a Muslim woman. I'm bringing everything I ever knew, and all the stories I've read – everything good, strong, kind and powerful. I bring it all with me into every situation, and I will not allow my life to be minimized by anybody's racism or sexism or ageism.

As far as I knew white women were never lonely, except in books. White men adored them, Black men desired them and Black women worked for them.

Don't hesitate to learn the most painful aspects of our history, understand it.

For Africa to me... is more than a glamorous fact. It is a historical truth. No man can know where he is going unless he knows exactly where he has been and exactly how he arrived at his present place.

History, despite its wrenching pain, cannot be unlived, but if faced with courage, need not be lived again.

I am overwhelmed by the grace and persistence of my people.

I have great respect for the past.

I would encourage us all, African Americans, Asians, Latinos, Whites, Native Americans to study history. I long for the time when all the human history is taught as one history. I am stronger because you are stronger. I am weaker if you are weak. So we are more alike than we are unlike.

I'm a descendant of someone bought and sold, and brought in 1619 in what was to become the United States.

It is imperative that young white men and women study the black American history. It is imperative that blacks and whites study the Asian American history.

It is time for parents to teach young people early on that in diversity there is beauty and there is strength.

My people couldn't have survived slavery without having hope that it would get better.

The country didn't get that way in a week; we've had years and years of getting behind in our economy. So President Obama stepped into a hellhole and people wanted him to change it as soon as he came in. But he's got his adversaries to deal with in the House and Senate, so it's not easy.

The fact that the adult American Negro female emerges a formidable character is often met with amazement, distaste and even belligerence. It is seldom accepted as an inevitable outcome of the struggle won by survivors, and deserves respect if not enthusiastic acceptance.

The problem I have with haters is that they see my glory, but they don't know my story.

There's racism and sexism and ageism and all sorts of idiocies. But bad news is not news. We've had bad news as a species for a long time. We've had slavery and human sacrifice and the holocaust and brutalities of such measure.

There's something beautiful about the fact that Obama was not just elected, but elected decisively across racial, and socio-economic and cultural groups and that we all celebrated in his win.

We all should know that diversity makes for a rich tapestry, and we must understand that all the threads of the tapestry are equal in value no matter what their color.

We are growing up. We are growing up! Out of the idiocies – the ignorances of racism and sexism and ageism and all those ignorances.

We cannot change the past, but we can change our attitude toward it. Uproot guilt and plant forgiveness. Tear out arrogance and seed humility. Exchange love for hate – thereby, making the present comfortable and the future promising.

Quotes about Justice and 'Doing the Right Thing'

I believe we are still so innocent. The species are still so innocent that a person who is apt to be murdered believes that the murderer, just before he puts the final wrench on his throat, will have enough compassion to give him one sweet cup of water.

I believe what I have to say is important, and I believe the people coming to hear me are important, and so the occasion of itself alone has an importance, which forces me to stare down my nerves.

I like to speak on matters which matter to human beings, and almost everything matters to human beings.

I pray for humility because that comes from inside out. And what humility does for one, is it reminds us that there are people before me. I have already been paid for. And what I need to do is prepare myself so that I can pay for someone else who has yet to come, but who may be here and needs me.

I wish that we could look into each other's faces, in each other's eyes, and see our own selves. I hope that the children have not been so scarred by their upbringing that they only think fear when they see someone else who looks separate from them.

In the 16th century, Niccolò Machiavelli – in an attempt to get back in the good graces of the powerful – wrote a slim volume called The Prince. In that book he showed the powers that be how to control the people. That book is a statement: separate and rule, divide and conquer. That's five hundred years ago and it still works, because we allow ourselves to be lead around with holes through our noses.

It is better to control oneself, if one can, and not hit back. But on certain occasions, it is imperative to defend oneself. I don't think it's fair to ask anybody not to defend herself or himself.

Let's tell the truth to people. When people ask, 'How are you?' have the nerve sometimes to answer truthfully.

My heart is so heavy when I see the reality of the Indian reservation and as an American, I know I am, too, responsible.

People trying to separate people rather than bring us together... please. You don't just see it in America. It's all over the world.

Prejudice is a burden that confuses the past, threatens the future and renders the present inaccessible.

The root cause of all the problems we have in the world today is ignorance of course. But most, polarization.

The truth is very important. No matter how negative it is, it is imperative that you learn the truth, not necessarily the facts. I mean, that, that can come, but facts can stand in front of the truth and almost obscure the truth. It is imperative that students learn the truth of our history.

The truth is, right may not be expedient. It may not be profitable, but it will satisfy your soul.

There's a world of difference between truth and facts. Facts can obscure the truth.

This is what I am learning, at 82 years old: the main thing is to be in love with the search for truth.

We allow our ignorance to prevail upon us and make us think we can survive alone, alone in patches, alone in groups, alone in races, even alone in genders.

While the rest of the world has been improving technology, Ghana has been improving the quality of man's humanity to man.

Selected Lines from Poems

Alone, all alone. Nobody, but nobody. Can make it out here alone.

I am a Woman. Phenomenally. Phenomenal Woman, that's me.

I couldn't tell fact from fiction, or if the dream was true. My only sure prediction in this world was you. I'd touch your features inchly. Beard love and dared the cost. The sented spiel reeled me unreal and I found my senses lost.

If one has courage, nothing can dim the light which shines from within.

Just do right. Right may not be expedient, it may not be profitable, but it will satisfy your soul. It brings you the kind of protection that bodyguards can't give you. So try to live your life in a way that you will not regret years of useless virtue and inertia and timidity. Take up the battle. Take it up. It's yours. This is your life. This is your world.

Out of the huts of history's shame, I rise. Up from a past that's rooted in pain, I rise. I'm a black ocean, leaping and wide. Welling and swelling I bear in the tide. Leaving behind nights of terror and fear, I rise. Into a daybreak that's wondrously clear, I rise. Bringing the gifts that my ancestors gave, I am the dream and the hope of the slave. I rise, I rise, I rise.

We need joy as we need air. We need love as we need water. We need each other as we need the earth we share.

When my bones are stiff and aching, and my feet won't climb the stair, I will only ask one favor: don't bring me no rocking chair. When you see me walking, stumbling, don't study and get it wrong. 'Cause tired don't mean lazy and every goodbye ain't gone. I'm the same person I was back then, a little less hair, a little less chin, a lot less lungs and much less wind. But ain't I lucky I can still breathe in.

Selected Quotes from Books and Literature

I KNOW WHY THE CAGED BIRD SINGS

Hoping for the best, prepared for the worst, and unsurprised by anything in between.

Life is going to give you just what you put in it. Put your whole heart in everything you do, and pray, then you can wait.

Words mean more than what is set down on paper. It takes the human voice to infuse them with deeper meaning.

MOM & ME & MOM

My mother's gifts of courage to me were both large and small. The latter are woven so subtly into the fabric of my psyche that I can hardly distinguish where she stops and I begin.

I will look after you and I will look after anybody you say needs to be looked after, any way you say. I am here. I brought my whole self to you. I am your mother.

I want you to learn that you cannot have anything without working for it.

Don't do anything that you think is wrong. Just do what you think is right, and then be ready to back it up even with your life.

THE COMPLETE COLLECTED POEMS OF MAYA ANGELOU

We are more alike, my friends, than we are unalike.

The caged bird sings with a fearful trill of things unknown but longed for still and his tune is heard on the distant hill for the caged bird sings of freedom.

A bird that stalks down his narrow cage can seldom see through his bars of rage his wings are clipped and his feet are tied so he opens his throat to sing.

A caged bird stands on the grave of dreams his shadow shouts on a nightmare scream his wings are clipped and his feet are tied so he opens his throat to sing.

AND STILL I RISE: A BOOK OF POEMS

You may shoot me with your words, you may cut me with your eyes, you may kill me with your hatefulness, but still, like air, I'll rise!

Had I known that the heart breaks slowly, dismantling itself into unrecognizable plots of misery... had I known yet I would have loved you, your brash and insolent beauty, your heavy comedic face and knowledge of sweet delights, but from a distance I would have left you whole and wholly for the delectation of those who wanted more and cared less.

You may write me down in history with your bitter, twisted lies. You may trod me in the very dirt, but still like dust, I'll rise.

THE HEART OF A WOMAN

You can't get too high for somebody to bring you down.

I had to trust life, since I was young enough to believe that life loved the person who dared to live it.

"Can I do it? I'd rather not try and fail". That's stupid talk Maya. Every try will not succeed. But if you're going to live, live at all, your business is trying...You fail, you get up and try again."

PHENOMENAL WOMAN: FOUR POEMS CELEBRATING WOMEN

Pretty women wonder where my secret lies. I'm not cute or built to suit a fashion model's size. But when I start to tell them, they think I'm telling lies. I say, it's in the reach of my arms the span of my hips, the stride of my step, the curl of my lips. I'm a woman. Phenomenally. Phenomenal woman, that's me.

Men themselves have wondered what they see in me. They try so much but they can't touch my inner mystery. When I try to show them they say they still can't see. I say, it's in the arch of my back, the sun of my smile, the ride of my breasts, the grace of my style. I'm a woman. Phenomenally. Phenomenal woman, that's me.

Now you understand just why my head's not bowed. I don't shout or jump about or have to talk real loud. When you see me passing it ought to make you proud. I say, it's in the click of my heels, the bend of my hair, the palm of my hand, the need of my care, 'cause I'm a woman. Phenomenally. Phenomenal woman, that's me.

I know that I'm not the easiest person to live with. The challenge I put on myself is so great that the person I live with feels himself challenged. I bring a lot to bear, and I don't know how not to.

LETTERS TO MY DAUGHTER

I can be changed by what happens to me, but I refuse to be reduced by it.

I believe that one can never leave home. I believe that one carries the shadows, the dreams, the fears and the dragons of home under one's skin, at the extreme corners of one's eyes and possibly in the gristle of the earlobe.

Make every effort to change things you do not like. If you cannot make a change, change the way you have been thinking. You might find a new solution.

All great artists draw from the same resource: the human heart, which tells us all that we are more alike than we are unalike.

One person, with good purpose, can, constitute the majority.